CLARENCE DARROW
"Attorney for the Damned"

BY GERALD KURLAND

B. A. Long Island University
M. A. Brooklyn College
Ph. D. The City University of New York

D. Steve Rahmas, A. B., J. D., Columbia U., Editor

Compiled with the assistance of the Research Staff of SamHar Press.

SamHar Press
Charlotteville, N.Y. 12036
A Division of Story House Corp.

1972

PRAIRIE STATE COLLEGE
LEARNING CENTER

Kurland, Dr. Gerald
    Clarence Darrow, Attorney for the Damned. Charlotteville, N.Y., Story House Corp. (SamHar Press), 1972.

    32 p. 22 cm. (Outstanding Personalities, no. 22)
    Bibliography: p. 32
    Story House Prebound

    1. Darrow, Clarence Seward, 1857–1938 2. Lawyers
(Series: Outstanding Personalities)

HN57.K8   923.4

(The above card has been cataloged by the editor and may not be identical to that of Library of Congress. Library card portrayed above is 80% of original size.)

Preassigned Library of Congress Catalog Card Number: 75-190240

Copyright © 1972   Story House Corp.,

All rights reserved. Printed in the United States of America.

CLARENCE DARROW
"Attorney for the Damned"

"The man who speaks the truth that is in him," Clarence Darrow declared while delivering the funeral oration for Governor John P. Altgeld, "although all the world hisses, is a sight of such moral grandeur that all mankind should bow down and honor him." Darrow's tribute to Altgeld, who earned the scorn of the community by doing what he felt was just, could easily be applied to himself. At the age of thirty-seven, Clarence Darrow turned his back on a promising career as a corporation lawyer-a career which undoubtedly would have brought him wealth and social prestige-in order to defend the scorned outcasts and the helpless poor of American society. He defended men and causes that were so unpopular that large segments of the public considered him to be a menace to the American way of life. And yet, the more he was castigated and condemned by polite society, the more dedicated he became to the cause of the downtrodden, and he launched a one man crusade to destroy the prejudice, parochialism, and callousness of his society. Clarence Darrow's biography is, in large measure, the history of twentieth century American jurisprudence, for he was involved in the most important and the most famous cases of the age-the Debs conspiracy, the Haywood murder trial, the McNamara case, the Leopold-Loeb case, and the Scopes Monkey Trial. After a long and stormy career, Clarence Darrow was acknowledged to be the greatest trial lawyer that America had ever produced. He was the "Attorney for the Damned," who defended those whom society had already condemned, and whom no other lawyer was willing to defend. Darrow spoke the truth that was in him without regard to the consequences, and continued his father's tradition of marching against the prevailing tide of public opinion. Often he defended unpopular causes for the sheer pleasure of upsetting the complacent.

AMIRUS DARROW The first Darrows came to America in the late-seventeenth century and settled as farmers in New England. The family never achieved any measure of worldly success and was always poor. Clarence's grandfather migrated to the Ohio frontier around 1830 in search of a better life for his family, but found only more hard work and poverty. His son, Amirus, was sent to school in Amboy where, it was hoped, he would acquire the education needed to free him from hard manual labor. In Amboy, Amirus fell in love with Emily Eddy, whose father had come to Ohio from Connecticut and who was prominent in the Underground Railroad which sought to aid Negro slaves to flee their bondage in the South. He married Emily at an early age, and the young couple went to Meadville, Pennsylvania where Amirus enrolled at Allegheny College. In addition to studying at Allegheny College, Amirus also attended a Unitarian seminary in Meadville, and was ordained a minister of the Unitarian Church. However, his study of philosophy and theology led him to doubt the existence of God, and he resigned from the Unitarian ministry becoming a life-long agnostic. After completing his studies, Amirus and his wife settled in Farmdale, Ohio, which was two miles from Kinsman. He was the only freethinker and one of the few Democrats in a community which was devoutly religious and overwhelmingly Republican. He was the proverbial "village atheist," and could always be counted upon to oppose the beliefs and mores of his neighbors. Not only was Amirus a minority of one, he was also extremely impractical. He earned his living by working as a carpenter, and ran a small furniture factory and undertaking business from the back of his house. However, he constantly neglected his work in order to read an interesting book, and worked only when it was unavoidable. The Darrow family was always poor and often had to skimp on the necessities of life, but Amirus' home was filled with hundreds upon hundreds of books and his children were never without intellectual nourishment. Emily struggled to provide for her eight children on a woefully inadequate budget, and worked herself to death when she was only forty-four.

CLARENCE The fifth child of Amirus and Emily Darrow, Clarence, was born on April 18, 1857 at the family home in Farmdale. In those years immediately preceding the Civil War Amirus ran the Kinsman, Ohio, branch of the Underground Railroad. In 1864 the Darrow family moved from Farmdale to the larger village of Kinsman where Clarence spent his formative years. Amirus demanded that his children pay strict attention to their studies, and Clarence, who was not a good student, was constantly called away from baseball and other games to do homework. Every Sunday, Emily took her children to Presbyterian Church services in Kinsman, although Amirus would have no part of it. However, he did not feel that he had the right to impose his prejudices on his children and wanted them to be exposed to all religious systems so that they could make up their own minds as to whether to believe or not to believe. Clarence, who was utterly repelled by the dogmatism of organized religion, embraced his father's agnosticism and also learned the meaning of tolerance. Throughout his life, he would defend the individual's right to believe what he wished, but would oppose all efforts to impose that belief on others. He did not feel that any individual or group had a monopoly on truth, but that all possessed some small part of it and that everyone should be permitted to find his own truth. As he grew older, Clarence helped his father in his furniture factory and helped with farm chores. He had a pet chicken which his mother slaughtered and cooked, and a horror-stricken Clarence not only refused to touch his dinner, but never ate another bite of chicken as long as he lived. Whenever he was invited to dinner, he would request that chicken not be served. Finally, Clarence Darrow played first base on the Kinsman baseball team, and one of the highlights of his life came when he won a game for his team with a ninth inning, two-out, home run. At sixteen, Clarence went to Meadville to attend Allegheny College.

A YOUNG MAN IN SEARCH OF HIMSELF Clarence did not really want to go to college and enrolled at Allegheny primarily because of family pressure. His older brothers and sisters helped pay his tuition, and he worked after school hours to meet his expenses. He detested Latin and Greek, which was still the core of the curriculum in many small American colleges, earned mediocre grades and "majored" in baseball which was still his first love. After completing his freshman year at Allegheny, the depression of 1873 struck America, and that provided him with the excuse he needed to leave college and return home. That summer Clarence worked in his father's furniture factory, and in the fall of 1873 he accepted a teaching position in the district school at Vernon, Ohio, which was not far from Kinsman. The academic credentials demanded of prospective teachers in late-nineteenth century America were quite modest, and the position was offered to Clarence because no other man would work for the low salary of $30 a month. He startled school authorities by abolishing the corporal punishment of unruly students and by throwing out McGuffey's readers (popular texts used in virtually every public school). He taught his classes directly from books borrowed from his father's library, and local parents feared that he would indoctrinate their children with unorthodox ideas. However, he had the virtue of working cheap, and that compensated for many faults. While Darrow enjoyed teaching and liked working with young people, he soon realized that he could not make teaching his career. It lacked the excitement and magnetism he was seeking in life, and he longed to match his wits and talent against men who were worldly and brilliant.

EXPANDING HORIZONS Darrow taught at Vernon for three years, during which time his intellect began to mature as he read widely in history, philosophy, science, and literature. He joined the Trumbull County debating society, and every Saturday night he matched his intellect and rhetorical ability against some of the finest minds in the county as he debated a wide range of philosophical, literary, and current topics. In 1875, at the age of eighteen, Clarence met a charming sixteen year old girl by the name of Jessie Ohl, began courting her and soon declared his love for her. In this period Darrow began reading law and grew ever more attracted to law as a career. The courtroom promised the clash of intellects and the excitement of battle which he longed for, but which he could not find in the classroom. His brother Everett, who was teaching in the Chicago public school system, and his sister Mary, who taught at Champagne, Illinois agreed to finance his legal education, and in 1876 Darrow entered the University of Michigan Law School at Ann Arbor. Again though, as at Allegheny College, he was a poor student, earned mediocre grades, and detested his classes. Darrow was a free spirit who resented the confinements of formal education, and after finishing his first year of law school he dropped out of the University of Michigan to become a clerk in a law office in Youngstown, Ohio.

AN ASPIRING YOUNG LAWYER Darrow spent one year reading law in Youngstown, Ohio, and learning legal procedures while working as a clerk. In 1878, at the age of twenty-one, he went before a panel of six lawyers who satisfied themselves that he knew the basic tools and principles of his trade, and they admitted him to the Ohio bar. Two years later, Clarence married his sweetheart of five years, and with Jessie's financial aid the couple settled in Andover, Ohio, where Darrow began his own legal practice. If he expected clients to flock to his office, he was disappointed. Little business came his way, and he earned barely enough to support himself and Jessie. For several years, he contented himself with drawing up wills, closing property sales, and representing local farmers in routine law suits. Slowly he began to build a modest practice, and shortly after the birth of his only child (Paul, who was born December, 1883), he moved to the larger town of Ashtabula in search of greater and more important business. In Ashtabula Darrow won the friendship of Judge Sherman who backed him for the post of city solicitor. As solicitor, Darrow represented the city of Ashtabula in law suits which involved the municipal government, and the position not only provided him with financial security but it also added to his professional prestige in the Ashtabula legal community. Not yet thirty years old, Darrow's intellect was still developing and maturing, and as his mind developed he became increasingly disenchanted with Ashtabula. He pursued a legal career because he yearned for the intellectual challenge which it afforded, but he became acutely aware that Ashtabula was a very small town which could not provide the challenge he craved. In 1887 he decided to seek his career in the big city, and he moved his family to Chicago where he could compete with the finest minds of the Mid-west.

CHICAGO He was to call Chicago his home for the remainder of his life, but upon his arrival he barely managed to earn his expenses. Since business was not coming to him, Darrow decided that he would have to seek out his clients. Accordingly, he joined the Henry George Single Tax Club which was dedicated to the eradication of poverty and social ills by taxing the unearned increment acquired by landowners and which was enjoying a vogue among middle class intellectuals. In addition Darrow joined the Sunset Club which was a literary society at whose meetings its members discussed the latest literary trends. He began writing literary essays, discovered that editors of literary magazines thought well enough of them to publish them, and supplemented his legal earnings with writing fees. For a half-century Darrow would find solace and escape in the writing of literary and topical essays and discovered that during times of crises, literary fees would keep him from impending bankruptcy. In 1888 Clarence Darrow campaigned for the Democratic party in the municipal and state-wide election campaign, and met John Peter Altgeld, the leader of the progressive wing of the Illinois Democratic party. A year later, Darrow established a local reputation in reform circles by participating in a campaign to force the Chicago streetcar companies to provide enough seats on their cars to eliminate the necesssity for passengers to stand during rush-hour trips. After campaigning for the election of DeWitt Cregier as Mayor of Chicago, Darrow, upon the recommendation of Altgeld, was appointed a special assessment attorney for the city of Chicago at a salary of $3000 per year. His duties were light, involving property tax disputes, and the salary provided him economic security. Politicians who came in contact with him liked his friendly easygoing approach and his inherent fairness, and after only three months as special assessment attorney Darrow was promoted to assistant corporation counsel at $5000 per year. Ten months later, Chicago's corporation counsel was forced to resign his office on account of ill health, and in 1890, at the age of thirty-three, Clarence Darrow found himself the chief legal counsel for the "windy" city.

BATTLING THE RAILROADS In the 1890's Chicago was the railroad crossroads of the United States, and the numerous railroads which started or terminated in Chicago were a potent political force in Illinois politics as well as a major holder of Chicago real estate. The city, however, was planning to hold a major world's fair in 1893 (the famous Columbian Exposition) and wanted to acquire some railroad rights of way in order to construct access roads to the fair site. The railroads, seeking to keep the access roads under their own control so that they could profit from the throngs of people who would attend the fair, refused to cooperate with the city authorities. Darrow, as Chicago's attorney, led the legal fight against the railroads and beat them in court where the condemnation powers of the city government were sustained. Not every lawyer possessed the skill to beat the railroads, and Darrow's feat was not lost upon the railroad men of Chicago who decided that they must have him on their side. In 1894 Darrow went to work for the Chicago and North Western Railroad at the handsome salary of $7000 per year. With his legal acumen, Darrow could have become one of the highest paid corporation lawyers in the country, but there were many things about corporate law which he did not like. He did not like the way the railroads conspired amongst themselves to fix rates, depress wages paid to employees, and limit competition. He did not like the blacklist by which the railroads conspired to deny employment to known union members; he opposed the use of Pinkerton detectives to spy on the railway unions; and he objected to the use of strikebreakers to smash unionization. Finally, he did not like the ways in which the railroads took advantage of woefully inadequate workman's compensation laws to cheat injured workmen of their just compensation. Darrow was able to persuade the Chicago and North Western to deal more liberally with its injured workmen than it had in the past, but even he could not remedy the many abuses which the company practiced. On the July 4th weekend of 1894 Darrow awoke to see federal troops marching down Chicago's streets to protect the railroads and break the strike being conducted by the American Railway Union. Unable to reconcile his duties with the Chicago and North Western with his social conscience, Darrow resigned his position with the railroad to defend the cause of organized labor, and began a new career that would see him become America's leading civil libertarian.

THE PULLMAN STRIKE Pullman, Illinois, was a Chicago suburb built by George Pullman to house his Pullman Palace Car Company. Everyone who worked for the company was required to live in Pullman and rent quarters from the Pullman Land Company and had to patronize company stores. Pullman, Illinois, was widely touted as the ideal factory town in which the workers had decent apartments and led wholesome lives. Actually, rents in Pullman were considerably higher than they were in adjoining communities, and rent money was deducted in advance from the worker's salary. Workers and their families were constantly spied upon by Pinkerton detectives, were forbidden from having liquor on their premises, and were forced to maintain their apartments to the satisfaction of George Pullman. In May, 1894, citing declining profits resulting from the depression of 1893, Pullman announced sweeping wage reductions. However, he refused to reduce rents and prices in the company stores to reflect the lower wage levels, and many workers wound up with as little as ten cents in cash after a week's work. On May 11, the Pullman workers went on strike. Ignoring pleas that he negotiate with Eugene V. Debs' American

Railway Union, which was representing the strikers, George Pullman remained adamant in his refusal to bargain with his employees. The American Railway Union called upon its members not to handle trains carrying Pullman cars, and the strike escalated. In July, the railroads persuaded Attorney General Richard Olney, who had close financial ties to the railroads, to send federal troops into Illinois for the ostensible purpose of protecting the mails. Olney's action, however, was unconstitutional. To this point there had been no violence in connection with the strike, and the post office was not reporting any substantial delays in mail delivery. Moreover, Governor Altgeld had not requested federal assistance, and the Constitution clearly states that federal troops can be sent into a state only at the request of its governor. The arrival of federal troops had the desired effect. Violence erupted, and the army troops were used as strikebreakers to smash the American Railway Union. Eugene V. Debs was arrested and charged with criminal conspiracy.

THE DEBS CONSPIRACY TRIAL   Clarence Darrow offered to defend Debs against the charge of criminal conspiracy, and his services were gladly accepted. The charge on which Debs was being tried grew out of the English common law which held that it was a conspiracy in restraint of trade for workmen to combine with one another for the purpose of raising their wages or lessening their hours of labor. Consequently, labor unions were deemed to be conspiracies in restraint of trade, and the advocacy of a strike constituted criminal conspiracy. It was an old doctrine which had been widely used in order to keep unions weak and harmless. When the trial began on January 26, 1895 before Judge Peter Grosscup, Darrow decided that his best defense would be a vigorous offense. He showed how the railroads conspired to fix rates and wages, and asked the jury why they were not indicted for conspiracy? He held that the law had an ingrained double standard, and that the criminal activities of the wealthy and the powerful went unpunished while the poor and weak were prosecuted to the full extent of the law. He subpoened George Pullman, but Pullman went into hiding to avoid

11

testifying at the Debs trial. Nevertheless, Darrow showed that during the 1893-1894 period when Pullman was crying poverty to justify his wage cuts the company was making a profit of $2,800,000. Demonstrating the conspiracy of the employers against their workers, Darrow came to the crux of his defense. Since it was perfectly legal, he argued, for an individual worker to refuse to work for the wage offered him, why was it illegal for a group of workers to voluntarily agree not to work for that same wage? In other words, how could it be illegal for two men to do what one man could legally do? Furthermore, with employers exercising such enormous economic power, the worker could improve his status only by cooperating with his fellow workers. The labor union then was the counterpart of the industrial corporation (in which capitalists combined with their fellows to obtain greater profits) and was every bit as lawful. Unfortunately, during the course of the trial, one of the jurors became seriously ill, and a mistrial had to be called. However, the jury was 11 to 1 in favor of acquittal, and realizing that it was beaten, the government declined to re-try Debs for criminal conspiracy. Instead, Debs was now charged with contempt for violating a federal injunction (no jury trial was required on a contempt citation) and was sentenced to six months imprisonment. Fate had cheated Darrow of the opportunity to establish the legal right of labor unions to strike.

CLARENCE DARROW, REFORMER The Debs case dramatically altered the course of Darrow's life and made him a spokesman for the poor and the weak. In 1895 he organized the firm of Collins, Goodrich, Darrow, and Vincent which specialized in corporate law. Since his labor and criminal clients could not pay him adequate fees, he needed a profitable law firm which would enable him to earn the income needed to finance his defense of the downtrodden. However, his partners objected to his handling labor and criminal cases, fearing that it would drive away business, and in 1897 the firm collapsed. Darrow immediately organized another firm with Edgar Lee Masters and Morris St. P. Thomas which lasted until 1911 and which represented a number of labor unions as well as William Randolph Hearst's Chicago *Evening American* (which was then a progressive newspaper catering to the masses). Darrow never turned anyone away, and from 1895-1900 it is estimated that between 1/3 and 1/2 of his clients were too poor to pay any fee. Darrow viewed crime as a social disease which was directly related to poverty and social injustice. He constantly complained that the crimes of the wealthy went unpunished while only the poor were sent to jail. Believing that crime was a disease, he felt that criminals should be treated as sick individuals and that the prime consideration should be to return them to society as useful members rather than mere punishment. In a series of essays published in the nation's leading periodicals, Darrow argued that man was a machine which responded to its external environment, and a criminal was a human machine which had broken down. It could best be repaired by changing the external environment (hence, eliminate poverty and social injustice) so that the cause of criminal behavior will have been eliminated. "I may hate the sin," Darrow declared, "but never the sinner." In his eyes criminals were no more to be blamed for their actions than victims of physical disease were to be blamed for their condition. Darrow's writings helped make American criminal law more humane, but his mechanistic interpretation of crime also served to reduce the individual's responsibility for his own actions. The fundamental difference between the criminal and the physically ill is that the criminal can choose not to be a criminal.

POLITICS AND DIVORCE By the mid-1890's Clarence Darrow was part of Chicago's intellectual establishment. His literary and legal essays established him as a leading voice of the rising liberal community, and he was constantly called upon to address a wide variety of reform groups. Unfortunately, Jessie Darrow was a homebody; she seldom read books, was unaware of contemporary social issues; and she disliked the people with whom her husband associated. As Darrow became a more important voice in Chicago civic life, he and Jessie saw less and less of each other. His legal work and his political activities kept him away from home for long periods of time. In 1896 Darrow let himself be persuaded to run for Congress on the Democratic ticket headed by John P. Altgeld. He campaigned against the use of federal troops in labor disputes and supported the free coinage of silver in order to inflate the currency and relieve the indebtedness of the nation's farmers. However, both he and Altgeld were hurt by the presidential candidacy of William Jennings Bryan, whose anti-industrial bias frightened capitalists and workers alike. Both went down to defeat, with Darrow losing by the close margin of 100 votes. Two years later, Darrow asked Jessie for a divorce after 18 years of marriage. He later came to regret the way in which he treated Jessie, but they parted amicably, and Darrow provided for her support until she remarried some years later. Meanwhile, in 1903, Darrow married Ruby Hamerstrom, who was 18 years his junior. Ruby was far more intellectually aware than Jessie, and Darrow's second marriage was a happy one.

THE KIDD CASE In 1900 Darrow had a second chance to defend labor against the charge of criminal conspiracy. Thomas I. Kidd led an unsuccessful strike of woodworkers in Oshkosh, Wisconsin, and was indicted for criminal conspiracy. In defending him Darrow used the same strategy and arguments that he had employed in the Debs case. He showed that the employers had hired child workers (in violation of state law) in order to replace adult workers and depress wages and that instead of paying their employees every week (as required by state law), they paid them once a month and had interest free use of their employees wages for three weeks out of every month. The workers, Darrow pointed out, had tried to reason with their employers, but they refused to correct abuses, leaving them with no alternative but to strike. The jury returned a verdict of "not guilty," and Darrow had won a major victory for organized labor. The use of the criminal conspiracy charge as an anti-union device was dealt a severe blow, and organized labor was partially freed of its judicial shackles.

ELECTED TO THE ILLINOIS LEGISLATURE Two years after the Kidd case, Darrow again ran for public office, and much to his dismay he was elected. He allowed himself to be talked into running for the Illinois Assembly on the Municipal Ownership ticket which had been formed to oppose Charles T. Yerkes' monopoly of the Chicago street railway system. In his drive for high profits, Yerkes had allowed service to deteriorate, and Chicago's reformers wanted the city to take over operation of the street cars in the hope that it would result in better service and lower fares. Capitalizing on public disgust with Yerkes, Darrow had won election to the Assembly, but before he could take his seat he received an urgent summons from United Mine Workers' President John Mitchell. All through the summer of 1902 anthracite coal workers had been on strike demanding higher wages, fewer working hours, and the correction of the abuses of the company store, whereby the mine owners had forced their employees to buy necessities at grossly inflated prices. The owners refused to negotiate with the miners, and with the approach of winter coal was becoming scarce, leading to fears of fuel shortages. Through the exertions of President Theodore Roosevelt, Senator Mark Hanna, and financier J.P. Morgan, both sides agreed to lay their case before an impartial commission whose award would be accepted as final and binding. The success of the strike and the fate of the union would depend on how effectively labor could present its case before the Anthracite Coal Commission, and Clarence Darrow was asked to plead labor's cause. Darrow showed how long hours in the mines destroyed the health of the miners, he demonstrated how the owners neglected safety standards in order to squeeze greater profits out of the mines, and he dramatically showed how the meager earnings of the miners were taken by the company stores which "mined the miners." "If you put a gun to a man's head," Darrow concluded, "and force him to give you ten cents to buy food, it is robbery. If the coal barons get all the coal in the world and let the people freeze, it is business." The commission awarded the miners a 10% across the board pay increase and additional increases geared to productivity. In addition, the length of the working day was cut from 10 hours to 9, but nothing was done to reform the abuses of the company stores. On the whole, though, the miners had won a significant victory, and Darrow was given much of the credit for it. In 1903, Darrow returned to Springfield, Illinois to assume his legislative duties. He helped pass legislation restricting the hours that child laborers could work and permitting municipal governments to expropriate and operate public utilities and transportation systems. He championed prison reform and was instrumental in establishing vocational training programs in the state prisons. Darrow declined to run for re-election to the Illinois Assembly in 1904. Instead, he went back to the practice of law.

THE WESTERN FEDERATION OF MINERS Among the most controversial and difficult cases of Darrow's career was his defense of the leaders of the Western Federation of Miners against the charge of murder. The federation had been organized back in 1902 by Big Bill Haywood as a militant union which advocated force and violence. In December, 1905, Idaho's ex-Governor Frank Steunenberg, who had crushed the Coeur d' Alene strike in 1899, was killed when a bomb exploded at the front gate of his home. Harry Orchard, a petty criminal who had worked briefly as a miner and who had acted as a spy for the mine owner's association, was arrested by Idaho authorities and charged with planting the bomb which killed Steunenberg. Orchard was thrown into solitary confinement, and James McParland, a Pinkerton detective in the employ of the mine owners, subjected him to a form of psychological torture and brainwashing. Orchard allegedly found God and decided to atone for his past sins by making a complete confession. He declared that Charles Moyer (President of the Western Federation of Miners), Big Bill Haywood (secretary-treasurer), and George Pettibone (a former W.F.M. official) had hired him to kill Steunenberg as well as several other prominent officials. Moyer, Haywood, and Pettibone were arrested by Pinkerton detectives without warrants and were taken from Colorado to Idaho without extradition papers (in short, they were kidnapped) where they were thrown in cells on death row at the Boise Penitentiary. Put in solitary, the three men were not permitted exercise periods and were denied warm clothing. At this point Clarence Darrow entered the case.

A TRIAL IN AN INSANE ASYLUM It was obvious that the mine owner's association was hoping to use Harry Orchard to destroy the Western Federation of Miners, and the lengths to which it went were simply incredible. When Darrow arrived in Boise, not only was he shunned by polite society, but he was constantly followed by Pinkerton detectives; his telephone was tapped; and his mail was opened. Since Moyer, Haywood, and Pettibone could not be convicted solely on the evidence of an accomplice, McParland needed someone to corroborate Orchard's confession. Accordingly, Steve Adams, a former W.F.M. official who was then a farmer in Oregon, was kidnapped and brought to Boise where he was given the choice of verifying Orchard's story or standing trial for the murder of a claim jumper in Wallace, Idaho. Adams had never killed anyone, but to avoid standing trial for murder he confessed to imaginary conspiracies. Darrow managed to contact Adams' family, and they persuaded him to repudiate his confession, promising that Darrow would defend him against the murder charge. Idaho put Adams on trial for murder to force him to testify against Moyer, Haywood, and Pettibone, but Darrow succeeded in getting a hung jury in Wallace, and the state's case was dealt a serious blow. Meanwhile, back in Boise, Darrow demanded that the charges against his clients be dismissed because they were illegally arrested. The motion was denied. According to the daughter of the presiding judge, "The whole procedure sounded as though it were taking place in an insane asylum." Once the trial began, Darrow showed that Orchard had a past record of perjury convictions, that he had a habit of confessing to crimes which he had not committed, and that he met Moyer, Haywood, and Pettibone only after he became a spy for the mine owner's association. The jury brought in a verdict of "not guilty," but the whole sorry episode had taken 18 months out of Darrow's life and exacted a heavy toll from his health.

A FREAK MASTOID In Boise, Darrow was under constant and relentless tension. He had never defended a man whom he believed to have been guilty, and he had no doubt that his three clients were innocent of the Steunenberg murder. But he discovered that Haywood was indeed guilty of numerous bombings and acts of violence, and he took an intense dislike to him. A man of peace and goodwill, Darrow abhorred violence, and the knowledge that his client had engaged in violent acts was a terrible psychological burden for him to bear. It probably contributed to the mastoid infection which struck him, and because of his many responsibilities to his clients, he was unable to have it treated properly. When the trial finally ended, the mastoid infection flared up, and Darrow was rushed to a California hospital where he nearly died. It took him a year and a half to recover his health and return to law practice. During his recuperation, he continued to write his essays and declared that, "I wish I could make the world kinder and more humane than it is." But he lamented, "People are getting more cruel all the time." In 1910 Darrow resumed his practice and was appointed a special counsel for the city of Chicago at $10,000 per year. He swore that he was through with labor cases.

THE MCNAMARA CASE On September 30, 1910, a bomb exploded at the Los Angeles *Times* building, killing 20 men. The *Times* was owned by Harrison Grey Otis (described by reformer Hiram Johnson as a man with a "gangrened heart and rotting brain"), who was leading the employer's drive to keep organized labor from getting a foothold in Los Angeles. The city was notorious for its hostility to labor unions, and the bombing was seen as a union attempt to settle accounts with Otis. James B. McNamara and Ortie McManigal were arrested in Detroit, Michigan, while John J. McNamara was picked up in Indianapolis. All three were officials of the International Bridge and Structural Iron Workers' Union, which had been attempting to organize Los Angeles; they were charged with the bombing and returned to California without proper warrants or extradition papers. The McNamara case appeared to be an exact repetition of the Moyer, Haywood, Pettibone case. "History repeats itself," Darrow quipped. "That's one of the things wrong with history." In any event, McManigal confessed to the crime, implicated the McNamaras and also admitted to planting over 100 bombs between 1906-1910. The McNamaras stoutly proclaimed their innocence, and Samuel Gompers (President of the American Federation of Labor) went to Darrow's Chicago apartment in the middle of the night to plead with him to defend the McNamaras. Darrow tried to decline, telling Gompers that such cases exacted a heavy personal toll and never repaid him for his labors. Gompers would not take "no" for an answer, and after several hours Darrow gave in and agreed to take the case. However, Darrow's law partners were vehement in their insistence that he not take the case, and when he stood by his promise to Gompers, they dissolved their partnership, leaving him without a source of income.

LOS ANGELES When Darrow arrived in Los Angeles, he found the atmosphere reminiscent of Boise, Idaho. However, the McNamaras had convinced organized labor and liberals that they were innocent, and the Socialist party was championing their cause in the hope that the popular backlash against the employers would carry them to the Los Angeles mayoralty. Indeed, as the year progressed, it seemed likely that the Socialists would sweep the city. Unfortunately, during the course of his investigations, Clarence Darrow discovered that his clients were guilty as charged and that the prosecution had enough evidence to hang them. "I can't stand to have a man I am defending hanged," Darrow cried out to an associate. "I can't stand it." Realizing that he had no chance of winning an acquittal, Darrow was willing to make a deal in order to spare the lives of his clients. Through the good offices of Lincoln Steffens, a liberal journalist, the prosecution agreed to drop the death penalty in return for a plea of guilty. They reasoned that such a plea would not only discredit the organized labor movement, but would scuttle the Socialist mayoral campaign. Without consulting the American Federation of Labor or informing the Socialists, Clarence Darrow rose in court late in November, 1911 and pled his clients guilty. The entire nation was shocked. James B. McNamara was given a life sentence, and John J. McNamara was sentenced to 15 years imprisonment. It was agreed that all criminal charges related to other bombings would be dropped. GET DARROW! When Darrow left the courtroom, the crowd which had gathered outside to follow the trial shouted, "Traitor! Traitor!" and hurled placards and garbage at him. Public revulsion to the McNamara case was so great that the Socialists were trounced in the December 5th Los Angeles mayoral election, and they blamed him for their defeat. To that point, the Socialists had considered Darrow as one of their own, and he was very sympathetic to their cause. Now, however, he was castigated, and the Socialists never again had a good word to say on his behalf. Moreover, organized labor considered him to be a traitor, and Gompers was so infuriated that he put him on his own personal blacklist. The McNamara case was the last labor case that Clarence Darrow handled; from then on every union in the country shunned him. However, the employers still considered Darrow a formidable enemy, and they were determined to destroy his career for all time. In January, 1912, a Los Angeles grand jury indicted him for attempting to bribe the McNamara jury. Darrow faced his greatest challenge. If convicted, his legal career would be at an end, and even if he were acquitted, his reputation might be damaged beyond the point of repair. His Socialist and labor friends had already turned their backs on him, and after the grand jury indictment many of his liberal middle class friends also abandoned him. Darrow was literally without a friend, and he was rapidly running out of funds.

AN INCREDIBLE TALE Bert Franklin was a former police official turned private detective, and Clarence Darrow hired him to investigate the backgrounds of prospective McNamara jurors, such investigations being routine procedures designed to discover jurors who might be personally biased against the defendants.

However, Franklin offered Robert Bain a downpayment of $500 and a final payment of $2,000 in return for a "not guilty" vote in the McNamara case. He made the same offer to George Lockwood, also a former policeman and a personal friend. Lockwood reported the offer to the authorities, and Franklin was caught in the act of passing the bribe money. The money had apparently been supplied by certain San Francisco labor unions, and Franklin had been hired by them to fix the jury. There was no indication that Clarence Darrow knew of the arrangement, much less that he approved of it. However, caught in the act, Franklin, in return for immunity from prosecution, agreed to testify that Darrow had put him up to it and had supplied the money. Ironically, it was Darrow who put up the bail money to have Franklin released from jail! Realizing that any lawyer who defended himself had a fool for a client, Darrow got Earl Rogers, California's most brilliant criminal lawyer, to defend him. Unfortunately, the two men quarreled over money and tactics, and towards the end of the trial Darrow took over his own defense. The *People vs. Clarence Darrow* took 90 days to try, and the emotional strain was so great that Ruby Darrow suffered a nervous breakdown.

VINDICATION Besides Franklin's testimony, the prosecution's case rested on payments which Darrow made to Franklin by check. Fortunately, Darrow's investigations were able to turn up witnesses who destroyed Franklin's credibility. John Drain and Frank Dominguez, two highly respected officials who were friends of Franklin, testified that immediately after his arrest Franklin declared that Darrow was the kindest man he had known and that he knew nothing of the bribe attempts. Four local reporters testified that they had heard Franklin make similar statements, and three of Franklin's associates declared that Franklin had admitted that he made a deal to save himself by getting Darrow. Darrow delivered his own summation, which lasted a day and a half, and a thousand people fought to get into the courtroom to hear it. He charged that the case against him was a deliberate contrivance developed by the Los Angeles employers who resented his constant defense of labor unions and radicals. He pointed out that he would not be so stupid as to hand out bribe money by check which could be traced back to him and that the checks made out to Franklin were payment for routine investigations of jurors. Besides, on the day that Franklin passed the bribe money, the deal to plead the McNamaras guilty had already been agreed upon, and Darrow pointed out that he would have no reason to bribe a juror when he knew that there would be no trial. His only crime, he insisted, was his defense of unpopular causes. It took the jury only twenty minutes to return a verdict of "not guilty," and Darrow's reputation was vindicated. But, the ordeal left him virtually bankrupt.

HOME After his acquittal, Darrow vowed that he would never again set foot on California soil (he never did), and he returned to Chicago as fast as he could to pick up the pieces of his shattered legal practice. He reopened his law office, but no clients sought his services. The corporations considered him to be a dangerous radical and wanted no part of him. The labor unions were still angry over the McNamara case, and they boycotted him. Middle class clients regarded him as too controversial, and they stayed away. Unable to earn a living as a lawyer, Darrow continued to write essays and went on the lecture circuit. Darrow proved to be a highly popular speaker, and he toured the Mid-west speaking before capacity audiences. His most popular topic was religion, and it was arranged for him to debate a priest, a minister, and a rabbi so that he could be sure of insulting all denominations. It was not unusual for Darrow to earn $1,000 for a single appearance, and he soon liquidated his debts. His lectures on religion established him as an American institution and as the heir to Robert Ingersoll who had been the nation's leading free thinker. He objected to religion's claim of having an absolute monopoly on truth, declaring that no man could be absolutely certain of the truth or falsehood of anything. He castigated theists of all faiths for looking for truth in a single book and neglecting the truths to be found in other books, and he condemned religion for setting man against man instead of bringing mankind closer together. Audiences which came to jeer Darrow found themselves half agreeing with him and left the lecture a good deal more humble than when they came. After two years on the lecture tour, Peter Sissman, who had once worked for Darrow, persuaded him to resume his practice and go into partnership with him. Sissman had a small criminal practice, and the first year of his partnership with Darrow left him with a smaller income than when he practiced on his own. Sissman actually lost business, but he felt that Darrow's was too great a talent to be lost to the legal profession and that by getting him back into practice he was making a contribution to society.

CRIMINAL LAW Once again Darrow found himself defending people who were too poor to pay for his services and who were in trouble with the law primarily because they were poor. However, as soon as he started winning cases, he attracted clients who could afford to pay, and by 1917 he was earning $30,000 a year and was acknowledged to be one of the best criminal lawyers in the country. When World War I broke out, Darrow was sympathetic to the Allied cause and supported the American war effort. But, as a civil libertarian, he defended those conscientious objectors who refused to participate in the war because of their religious or ethical beliefs. Darrow did not feel that a democratic society had the right to force any individual to perform an act against his conscience, even if the refusal to perform that act endangered the existence of that society. In most cases, the courts did not accept Darrow's reasoning.

DEFENDING THE RADICALS 1919 was the height of the Red Scare when many people became convinced that America was in imminent danger of being taken over by Bolshevik revolutionaries. Darrow was in the vanguard of those who urged a return to reason and a scrupulous defense of civil liberties. In Milwaukee, 11 Italian anarchists were sentenced to 25 years in prison for allegedly blowing up a police station. No explosives were found in their possession, and there was no evidence connecting them with the crime. However, they were known anarchists, and they had distributed literature urging the violent overthrow of the government and acts of terrorism against public officials. On the basis of that evidence they were convicted. Darrow took charge of their appeal. He argued that they were convicted for their beliefs, not for their actions, and that there was absolutely no evidence that they had translated their preachments into overt acts. All eleven were freed. In Rockford, Illinois, Darrow defended Arthur Person and 10 fellow Communists who were charged with attempting to violently overthrow the United States Government. Again, he argued that the Constitution's guarantee of freedom of speech gave Americans the right to advocate the violent overthrow of government and that only overt action, and not rhetoric, could be punished by law. In this case Darrow won an acquittal; however, he did not win all his cases. In Chicago, William Bross Lloyd, son of reformer Henry Demarest Lloyd, and sixteen other intellectuals were arrested for advocating the overthrow of the United States Government. All received sentences of 1 to 2 years in jail as the jury ignored Darrow's plea that advocacy of the violent overthrow of government was protected by the First Amendment. Gradually the Red Scare subsided, and the American people returned to their senses. Clarence Darrow had helped to prevent the use of the American legal system as a club with which to suppress unpopular points of view and had helped to preserve the civil liberties of all Americans.

LEOPOLD-LOEB The Leopold-Loeb case is probably the most famous murder trial of the twentieth century, and as the attorney for the defense, Clarence Darrow became a household word and endured some of his most bitter criticism. Nathan Leopold, Jr., and Richard Loeb were respectively 19 and 18 years old in 1924. Both were the sons of wealthy Jewish families; both were brilliant (Leopold graduated from the University of Chicago at 18, Loeb from the University of Michigan at 17); and both were mentally ill. Leopold had been shy and friendless as a child; he suffered from various glandular deficiencies which affected his personality and mind. An adherent of the philosophy of Friedrich Nietzsche, Leopold was convinced that he was a Nietzschian superman-an individual of superior intellect who was above the laws and morality of society and who was a law unto himself. All he needed was the chance to prove his superiority over his fellow man. Loeb, on the other hand, was raised by a strict governess whom he delighted in deceiving. He became an adept liar and cheater, and as a child, he would fantasize that he was a master criminal. Nathan Leopold was an ideal partner in crime for Richard Loeb and together they performed a number of petty robberies and committed numerous acts of malicious mischief. Loeb, however, dreamed of committing the perfect crime, and Leopold wanted to prove that he and Loeb were supermen. During the summer of 1924, they agreed to commit the ultimate and the perfect crime. They would commit murder. Fourteen year old Robert Franks (Loeb's own cousin) was selected as the victim. He was repeatedly stabbed with an ice pick and his body dumped in an isolated area. There was absolutely no motive for the killing; it was done simply for the thrill of it. It so happened that Leopold lost his eyeglasses in the vicinity of the dumping area, and the police were able to trace them back to him. Under police questioning, Loeb broke down and confessed the crime.

IN DEFENSE OF THE INDEFENSIBLE The entire nation was shocked and outraged by the senseless crime, and the people of Illinois loudly demanded the death penalty for the accused killers. The families of Leopold and Loeb pleaded with Clarence Darrow to take the case not to win an acquittal, but merely to save their sons' lives. It was rumored that they had promised him a million dollar fee. Actually, when Darrow agreed to take the case no fee was mentioned, and he told the families that he would let the Bar Association fix his fee so that he would not be accused of selling out to the rich. Darrow took the case not for the money, but because he believed that the rich had the same rights as the poor to good legal counsel (after all, he declared, "the rich have rights, too"), and because he had long opposed capital punishment. According to Darrow, capital punishment was absolutely useless as a deterrent to crime, and the greatest of all crimes was the deliberate taking of life by society. Capital punishment, he believed, cheapened the value of life and destroyed its sanctity. The sight of the state taking life only promoted more brutality and more barbarism in society. The state, he felt, must set the example and show that all life was sacred by its precept, not its preachments. For these reasons, he agreed to take the case and try to defend the indefensible. But many people accused Darrow of selling out his convictions, of turning his back on the people who needed him most, and of taking the case merely for the large fee. In defending Leopold and Loeb he met the same hostility that he had encountered in Boise and Los Angeles. People keep making the mistake of assuming that a lawyer necessarily approves the acts committed by the clients he is defending. But a lawyer defending a killer no more favors murder than a doctor who treats the ill favors disease. THE TRIAL Realizing that he could never hope to get an unprejudiced jury and that his clients were guilty as charged, Darrow pleaded them guilty but told Judge Caverly that he intended to produce evidence of mitigating circumstances. In this way Darrow avoided the necessity of a jury trial and made the presiding judge alone responsible for sentencing his clients to death. As he told Judge Caverly in his summation, he could not shift responsibility for the death sentence on the jury, and if he imposed it, he would have to do so with cold-blooded and deliberate intent. Darrow was gambling that Caverly could not condemn his fellow man to death. In his argument of mitigating circumstances Darrow broke new legal ground. He did not claim that his clients were insane, but instead maintained that they were mentally ill and that therefore they were not fully responsible for their actions. Up to this point, a criminal defendant was either sane or insane, there being no middle ground. Darrow's argument of diminished responsibility was a revolutionary legal doctrine which was used many times in subsequent years and which is now generally acknowledged to be a mitigating circumstance. His summation took three full days and is one of the most eloquent pleas ever made in any courtroom. "I am pleading," he declared, "that we schian superman—an individual of superior intellect who was above the laws and morality of society and who was a law unto himself. All he needed was the chance to prove his superiority over his fellow man. Loeb, on the other hand, was raised by a strict governess whom he delighted in deceiving. He became an adept liar and cheater, and as a child, he would fantasize that he was a master criminal. Nathan Leopold was an ideal partner in crime for Richard Loeb and together they performed a number of petty robberies and committed numerous acts of malicious mischief. Loeb, however, dreamed of committing the perfect crime, and Leopold wanted to prove that he and Loeb were supermen. During the summer of 1924, they agreed to commit the ultimate and the perfect crime. They would commit murder. Fourteen year old Robert Franks (Loeb's own cousin) was selected as the victim. He was repeatedly stabbed with an ice pick and his body dumped in an isolated area. There was absolutely no motive for the killing; it was done simply for the thrill of it. It so happened that Leopold lost his eyeglasses in the vicinity of the dumping area, and the police were able to trace them back to him. Under police questioning, Loeb broke down and confessed the crime.

IN DEFENSE OF THE INDEFENSIBLE The entire nation was shocked and outraged by the senseless crime, and the people of Illinois loudly demanded the death penalty for the accused killers. The families of Leopold and Loeb pleaded with Clarence Darrow to take the case not to win an acquittal, but merely to save their sons' lives. It was rumored that they had promised him a million dollar fee. Actually, when Darrow agreed to take the case no fee was mentioned, and he told the families that he would let the Bar Association fix his fee so that he would not be accused of selling out to the rich. Darrow took the case not for the money, but because he believed that the rich had the same rights as the poor to good legal counsel (after all, he declared, "the rich have rights, too"), and because he had long opposed capital punishment. According to Darrow, capital punishment was absolutely useless as a deterrent to crime, and the greatest of all crimes was the deliberate taking of life by society. Capital punishment, he believed, cheapened the value of life and destroyed its sanctity. The sight of the state taking life only promoted more brutality and more barbarism in society. The state, he felt, must set the example and show that all life was sacred by its precept, not its preachments. For these reasons, he agreed to take the case and try to defend the indefensible. But many people accused Darrow of selling out his convictions, of turning his back on the people who needed him most, and of taking the case merely for the large fee. In defending Leopold and Loeb he met the same hostility that he had encountered in Boise and Los Angeles. People keep making the mistake of assuming that a lawyer necessarily approves the acts committed by the clients he is defending. But a lawyer defending a killer no more favors murder than a doctor who treats the ill favors disease. THE TRIAL Realizing that he could never hope to get an unprejudiced jury and that his clients were guilty as charged, Darrow pleaded them guilty but told Judge Caverly that he intended to produce evidence of mitigating circumstances. In this way Darrow avoided the necessity of a jury trial and made the presiding judge alone responsible for sentencing his clients to death. As he told Judge Caverly in his summation, he could not shift responsibility for the death sentence on the jury, and if he imposed it, he would have to do so with cold-blooded and deliberate intent. Darrow was gambling that Caverly could not condemn his fellow man to death. In his argument of mitigating circumstances Darrow broke new legal ground. He did not claim that his clients were insane, but instead maintained that they were mentally ill and that therefore they were not fully responsible for their actions. Up to this point, a criminal defendant was either sane or insane, there being no middle ground. Darrow's argument of diminished responsibility was a revolutionary legal doctrine which was used many times in subsequent years and which is now generally acknowledged to be a mitigating circumstance. His summation took three full days and is one of the most eloquent pleas ever made in any courtroom. "I am pleading," he declared, "that we overcome cruelty with kindness and hatred with love." In delivering his verdict Judge Caverly did not address himself to Darrow's argument that mental illness constituted a mitigating circumstance. Instead, he sentenced Leopold and Loeb to life imprisonment solely on the grounds that they had pled guilty and that they were still minors. It was against the conscience of the court to sentence minors to death, and on that basis their lives were spared. Darrow had accomplished the purpose for which he had been hired, but months passed, and he received no word from the families concerning his payment. He wrote several letters requesting that his fee be settled, but the Leopolds and Loebs appeared reluctant to pay anything. Finally, he was presented with a check for $100,000 and was told that that was all the families intended to pay. After deducting the costs of his expenses, Darrow's share for defending Leopold and Loeb came to only $30,000. The Bar Association declared the fee to be inadequate, and advised Darrow to sue, but he refused, declaring that it would only make it appear that he had taken the case for the money.

THE SCOPES MONKEY TRIAL One year after Leopold-Loeb, Clarence Darrow became a leading protagonist in a trial that was equally famous, but far more humorous. The state of Tennessee, under pressure from Protestant Fundamentalists who were especially strong in the South, passed a law forbidding the teaching in the public schools of any subject or theory which conflicted with the Biblical account of man's development and history. The law was aimed against the teachings of modern science, particularly the Darwinian theory of evolution, and was designed to preserve the innocent faith of a simple age from the complexities of the modern world. However, the Tennessee law was not only an infringement of constitutional liberties; it also held the state up to derision throughout the civilized world, and civil libertarians were determined to challenge its constitutionality. John T. Scopes, a biology teacher in Dayton, Tennessee, agreed to become a test case and violated the law by teaching the theory of evolution. He was arrested, and the state moved to prosecute him for violating the anti-evolution law. At this point, William Jennings Bryan, the acknowledged champion of the Fundamentalist movement, volunteered to help the prosecution. Bryan's services were not wanted, as state authorities did not want to magnify a situation that was already embarrassing, but there was no way to turn him down without inviting severe political repercussions. When it was announced that Bryan would be a part of the prosecution, the American Civil Liberties Union, the attorney for Scopes, requested the aid of Clarence Darrow, who warmed to the challenge and offered his services without fee. The stage was set for one of the most dramatic confrontations in American legal history, a confrontation familiar to millions of Americans who saw the play and movie versions of *Inherit the Wind* which was based on the Scopes case.

"YOUR OLD MAN'S A MONKEY" When Darrow arrived in Dayton, Tennessee in the summer of 1925, he entered a town jammed with visitors coming to see the trial-a town in which a carnival atmosphere prevailed. On literally every corner, itinerant Fundamentalist preachers were haranguing crowds, and peddlers were selling Bibles and religious artifacts. Signs blazoned from countless buildings urging people to seek God and resist the allure of atheists like Darrow. When he walked the streets of Dayton, old ladies cursed him as that "damned infidel." Finally, the trial began with Judge John Raulston presiding, and Darrow exploded a number of bombshells. He objected to the court's being opened with a prayer (which was absolutely unheard of in the United States) and was overruled. He asked that a large "Read Your Evolution" placard be placed next to the "Read Your Bible" sign displayed above the entrance to the court. That request was also denied, although Judge Raulston did order the removal of the "Read Your Bible" sign. Finally, Darrow demanded that the case against Scopes be dismissed on the grounds that the Tennessee law violated the First Amendment guarantees of the Constitution. Raulston refused to take the responsibility of ruling the law unconstitutional, and the trial was allowed to proceed. In his defense of Scopes Darrow planned to call leading theologians of all faiths who would testify that there was no contradiction between science and religion. He also intended to call leading scientists, anthropologists, and historians who would testify to the validity of the evolutionary theory, who would trace the development of man, and who would show how his intellect and conception of the universe had grown over the centuries. Bryan, however, objected that Darrow's witnesses were irrelevant, immaterial, and incompetent, and Judge Raulston ruled in his favor. For the first time in his legal career, Darrow lost his temper and assailed the incredible ignorance and prejudice of Bryan and the court. And, for the first time in his life, he was cited for contempt of court. Since he could not call his expert witnesses, Darrow decided to question Bryan as an expert on the Bible in the hopes that he could show the world how ridiculous the beliefs of the Fundamentalists were.

Darrow maneuvered Bryan into declaring that he believed every word of the Bible to be literally true-a statement that no intelligent Christian would make. He began questioning Bryan on the story of the creation and asked him when the Flood occurred. "I never made a calculation," Bryan responded. "What do you think?" Darrow asked. "I do not think about things I don't think about," he retorted. "Do you think about things you do think about?" Darrow inquired as laughter welled up from the audience. As the questioning went on, Bryan looked more and more absurd, and the Fundamentalists realized that they were being made to look like monkeys. He asked Bryan if he believed that the serpent was made to crawl on its belly as punishment for tempting Eve. When Bryan said that he did, Darrow asked him how the serpent went about before he tempted Eve, "Do you suppose he walked on his tail?" Again, the audience broke into laughter. By the time the questioning was over, Bryan had been literally destroyed, and he died shortly after the end of the trial. Scopes was fined $100, and the case promptly appealed. The fine was thrown out on a technicality, but Darrow and the A.C.L.U. failed to have the law declared unconstitutional.

THE SWEET CASE No sooner had Darrow finished his business in Dayton than he was implored to defend Dr. Ossian Sweet, a Negro dentist who had bought a house in a white neighborhood of Detroit, Michigan, and who was being tried for murder along with ten other Negroes. Darrow had always defended Negroes in trouble with the law because he regarded them "as the underdogs under the underdogs," and he readily consented to take the case. Dr. Sweet had been warned not to try to move into his new house. Expecting trouble, he took possession of his home equipped with ten guns and 400 rounds of ammunition and accompanied by ten friends and relatives. That night a crowd of some 500 angry whites gathered in front of the Sweet house and threw rocks, knocking out all the windows. Dr. Sweet and his associates were in panic, convinced that the mob would attempt to storm the house and lynch them. When a group of whites approached their front lawn, the Negroes opened fire, killing one man and wounding another. The police promptly arrested them, and the authorities charged all eleven with first degree murder claiming that the police had the crowd under control and that there was no danger that the Sweet house would be stormed. Darrow sought to convince the jury that the Negroes were sincerely concerned for their physical safety, and he recited the history of white attacks on Negroes. He showed that Sweet and his friends had witnessed the lynchings of Negroes when they were children, and argued that their homicide was justifiable in view of the psychological terrors of mob action. After three days and nights of deliberations, the jury was unable to reach a verdict and a hung jury was declared. The state declined to re-try all eleven Negroes, and instead retried only Henry Sweet (Dr. Sweet's brother) who had actually fired the shots. At that trial, Darrow won an acquittal and established an important civil rights precedent-that a man had the right to buy the home of his choice and defend it against a hostile mob.
FINAL YEARS Darrow was now approaching his seventieth birthday, and the physical strain of a busy law practice was becoming too much for him. Consequently, he went into a semi-retirement, and during the last

decade of his life, he defended only one case of note. In 1932, Darrow went to Honolulu, Hawaii, to defend Navy Lieutenant Massie who had killed one of the five Hawaiians who had raped his wife after a local jury had refused to convict the men she identified as her attackers. The case had become a racial issue, and an Oriental jury had refused to convict fellow Orientals. Despite Darrow's defense, Massie was sentenced to 10 years for manslaughter, but was pardoned by the territorial governor before he had served any time. Increasingly, though, Darrow turned to writing as the major activity of his last years. In the *Prohibition Mania*, he condemned national prohibition as an infringement of the personal liberties of the individual and as an odious device which trampled respect for law and encouraged a lawlessness sanctioned by public opinion. Similarly, in *Infidels and Heretics*, he attacked the bigotry and parochialism of organized religion and defended the individual's right to seek truth wherever he wished. In 1934 Darrow was appointed Chairman of the National Recovery Administration's Review Board which was charged by President Roosevelt with investigating alleged inequities of the N.R.A. Condemning the N.R.A. for favoring the trusts at the expense of small businessmen, he called for an end to price fixing and for increased Federal Trade Commission jurisdiction over trusts which abused their powers and exploited the people. His report was instrumental in persuading President Roosevelt to abandon the N.R.A. as a failure and to seek industrial recovery in other ways. After a long and debilitating illness Clarence Darrow died on March 13, 1938, at the age of eighty-one.

Darrow spent most of his adult life fighting for the rights of labor, the freedom of the individual, and a more humane code of law. Unlike his latter-day counterparts who defend unpopular men and causes, he never found it necessary to impede the judicial process or frustrate the normal workings of the law by indulging in courtroom hysterics and disruptions. Indeed, he was convinced that the working man would advance, the individual become freer, and society more just and humane only by respecting the law, working within its confines, and using it to bring social justice in an orderly manner. The law was his instrument for creating a better world, and he never abused it.

BIBLIOGRAPHY

BY DARROW: Darrow published a considerable body of work, beginning with *A Persian Pearl* (1899), a collection of his literary essays. *Resist Not Evil* (1904) was a collection of essays on social, political, and legal questions; while *An Eye for an Eye* (1905) was a novel expressing his conviction that poverty and social injustice was responsible for criminal behavior; and *Farmington* (1905) was a recollection of his childhood in Farmdale and Kinsman, Ohio. *Crime, Its Causes and Treatment* (1925) embodies Darrow's mature thought on the subject; while *The Prohibition Mania* (with Victor S. Yarros) (1927) condemned the effort to regulate private morality; and *Infidels and Heretics* (with Walter Rice) (1927) expressed Darrow's negative attitudes toward religion. *Story of My Life*, Darrow's autobiography was published in 1932. In addition, Darrow published a large number of pamphlets and newspaper and magazine articles which are conveniently listed in the bibliography of Irving Stone's *Clarence Darrow for the Defense* (1941).

BIOGRAPHIES: The standard biography is Irving Stone's previously cited *Clarence Darrow for the Defense* (1941) which supersedes Charles Y. Harrison's *Clarence Darrow* (1931), and Allen Crandall's *The Man from Kinsman* (1933). The most recent biography is Miriam Gurko's *Clarence Darrow* (1965) which is an able brief treatment.

SPECIAL STUDIES: For an analysis of Darrow as a writer see Abe C. Ravitz, *Clarence Darrow and the American Literary Tradition* (1962). Convenient collections of Darrow's courtroom addresses and other writings are Arthur Weinberg (ed.), *Attorney for the Damned* (1957); Arthur Weinberg (ed.), *Verdicts Out of Court* (1963); and Marcet Haldeman-Julius, *Darrow's Two Great Trials* (1927). A number of Darrow's more important cases have been the subject of special treatments, see especially: Leslie H. Allen, *Bryan and Darrow at Dayton* (1967); Alexander Irvine, *Revolution in Los Angeles* (1911); Alvin V. Sellers, *The Loeb-Leopold Case* (1926); and William T. Stoll, *Tennessee Evolution Trial* (1925). Fremont Wood's *Moyer, Haywood, Pettibone and Harry Orchard* (1931) is an able treatment of the Steunenberg case.

ADDITIONAL BIOGRAPHY: *Ten Heroes of the Twenties* (1966) by Rex Lardner.